We enter this prayer, fasting,
inal victory. We join him in patience and hope as we walk through
0 days of personal discipline over the flesh, the world, and the devil.

Through prayer, we elevate our mind toward God - our consciousness, houghts, perceptions, perspectives, and intellectual abilities. We promote our heart - our passions, feelings and emotions, desires, ind longings.

Through fasting, we break our attachment to physical and material hings, freeing the soul from secondary things and reminding ourselves of what's essential.

Through acts of charity, we free ourselves from self-centeredness, ostering love, care, and concern for others. We remind ourselves of our responsibility for the common good, our responsibility to the most vulnerable and those in need in our society.

This book is a collection of devotional readings and reflections around themes of Lent to assist you in this brief season of renovating our interior life.

admonish you to be strong and very courageous, for you will emerge in the power of the Spirit, ready for the year ahead.

Pastor A. R. Bernard
Christian Cultural Center

CHRISTIAN
CULTURAL
C E N T E R

Day 1

Ash Wednesday

An Audience of One

Minister Mischa Field

Today's Reading
Matthew 6:1-21

"For where your treasure is, there your heart will be also."
— Matthew 6:21 (NIV)

Having pure motives is hard. We try to do good things. We try to do the right thing. Eventually, we may receive attention for it. Acknowledgment might be part of our motivation: *Look at me doing good things!* We may start with pure intentions but get addicted to praise until praise becomes our favorite thing. The good deeds can even become our identity: *Now I'm doing MY thing.* And quickly, our desire to do the right thing succumbs to a longing to be *seen* doing the right thing.

Jesus repeatedly warns against self-seeking. In Matthew 6:1, Jesus said, "Be careful not to practice your righteousness in front of others to be seen by them. If you do, you will have no reward from your Father in heaven" (NIV). He said serving for an audience is *self*-serving.

COURAGEOUS SACRIFICE
A LENTEN DEVOTIONAL

CHRISTIAN CULTURAL CENTER

LIONLAB

Courageous Sacrifice
A Lenten Devotional
by
Christian Cultural Center

ISBN: 979-8-8691-5055-4

Lionlab Publishing
lionlab.net

1 2 3 4 5   28 27 26 25 24

Introduction

Pastor A. R. Bernard

L ent is a time of reflection that brings us a more profound aware-
ness of God's presence in our lives. During this time of prayer,
fasting, and giving, we draw nearer to Christ in a special way, dis-
cerning His providence and purpose for us and His vision for humanity.

The focus of the Lenten Season is the cross, a symbol of selfless love
and courageous sacrifice. The triumphal entry into Jerusalem,
where they shouted Hosanna to the Son of David; the cleansing of
the temple where he expressed his zeal for the place where heaven
and earth were supposed to meet; the intimate Last Supper with
his disciples, where he called them friends and revealed the true
meaning of the Passover; the agony in the garden, his arrest, trial,
crucifixion, and death; all grip our hearts with remembrance of
God's supreme act of love to save fallen humanity.

Through it all, he kept his peace, thus declaring himself the Lord of
discipline, patience, and hope. However, the story of Christ's
Passion ends not with death and failure but with the power of his
resurrection, victory over sin, death, and the grave.

Don't give, pray, or fast for an audience.

True fasting should include setting the oppressed free, feeding the hungry, sheltering and clothing the poor, and not ignoring the needs of people we are related to by blood or common humanity (Isaiah 58:6-7).

Wrong-hearted fasting expects material reward and leaves our violent and unjust ways untouched. Sure, we skipped lunch, but we're still vicious, dishonest, and cruel.

Who are you trying to please with your fasting, your choices, and your service? What are you hoping to gain? Jesus' answer is for believers to do everything for an audience of one: God. Trust that He will reward you. However, you will not experience your full recompense on this side of glory.

Focus on the Lord as your only motivation; the fulfillment from a heart in line with God will be reward enough.

Additional Reading

Isaiah 58:1-12   2 Corinthians 5:20b-6:10   Psalm 103

Father, May my service honor You. May my prayers reach You. May my sacrifices remain between You and me. And may You be pleased with me.

I pray, in Jesus' Name. Amen.

Day 2

Thursday After Ash Wednesday

True Discipleship

Minister Adam Durso

Today's Reading
Luke 9:19-25

"But what about you?" he asked. "Who do you say I am?"
— Luke 9:20 (NIV)

The path of true discipleship is not an easy one, for it demands both conviction and sacrifice. Jesus, in His teachings, emphasized the essence of true discipleship - a willingness to forsake worldly desires and comforts to follow Him wholeheartedly. As we embark on this sacred Lenten journey, let us take a moment to pause and reflect on the words of our Savior. He calls us to lay down our ambitions and desires, surrendering them at the foot of the cross. In this act of surrender, we find the true essence of discipleship.

To be a disciple means more than simply sharing the Good News with others through spoken words. It requires us to become vessels of God's love and truth, reflecting His character in all we do. Each action, each word spoken, should be a testament to the transformative power of Christ's presence in our lives.

True discipleship calls us to make sacrifices. It beckons us to relinquish the comfortable familiarity of our routines and step into unknown territories to follow Him. It may mean abandoning material possessions that hold us captive or leaving behind relationships that hinder our spiritual growth. These sacrifices are not made in vain but rather pave the way for a deeper intimacy with our Savior.

Let this Lenten season be a time of deep introspection. In the silence of our hearts, may we ask ourselves how far we are willing to go in our discipleship journey. Are we ready to lay down our pride and ambitions at the feet of Jesus? Are we willing to embrace discomfort as we follow Him on the narrow path?

Additional Reading
Deuteronomy 30:15-20   Psalm 1

Lord, As I navigate through the season of Lent, grant me the wisdom to embrace sacrificial living. Help me understand that surrendering my desires means I find true life in You. Amen.

Day 3

Friday After Ash Wednesday

A Focused Sacrifice

Minister Malissa Redmond

Today's Reading
Matthew 9:10-17

"No, this is the kind of fasting I want: Free those who are wrongly imprisoned; lighten the burden of those who work for you. Let the oppressed go free, and remove the chains that bind people."
— Isaiah 58:6 (NLT)

Living in a time when people are quick to judge based on limited information has often led to presumptions and inaccurate judgments. The time needed to find the truth about a person or situation requires unbiased discernment; sadly, many of us are quick to slap on labels without a moment's thought that we may have misinterpreted the signs. Author Bonnie Lyn Smith advises, "Ask if you need to, but don't assume. Sometimes our bad feelings are only assumptions and speculations doing dark dances in our heads."[1] If you were to see a church member in the company of the town drunk, where would your mind go? Jesus was faced with that type of judgment from the Pharisees.

In Matthew 9:10-17, we have a glimpse of Jesus being about the Father's business in the company of well-known exploiters and niquitous individuals. Religious leaders poorly assessed the reason or the gathering, assuming He couldn't have a good motive for being with those types of people. The Lord responded to their questions with laser-focused clarity, confidence, and correction, saying, "Those who are healthy have no need for a physician, but [only] those who are sick. Go and learn what this [Scripture] means: 'I desire compassion [for those in distress], and not [animal] sacrifice,' for I did not come to call [to repentance] the [self-proclaimed] righteous who see no need to change], but sinners [those who recognize their sin and actively seek forgiveness]" (Matthew 9:12-13, AMP).

esus sacrificed His reputation to offer forgiveness to those in need regardless of the backlash. He refused to conform to the pressure within the culture to avoid certain people because people were His purpose. Do you recognize the same to be true for you? Stay focused on your assignment. You will certainly face significant challenges; however, stay the course, finish well, and never hesitate to offer grace to those in need.

Additional Reading

Isaiah 58:1-9   Psalm 51:1-10

Lord, I come to You asking for help understanding my purpose and sharing Your message. Even those people with unfavorable reputations, help me communicate truth in love without compromising. In Your Name I pray, Amen.

Day 4

Saturday After Ash Wednesday

What's the Point?

Minister Paul H. Coty, III

Today's Reading
Luke 5:27-32

*"Jesus answered them, 'It is not the healthy who need a doctor,
but the sick.'"*
— Luke 5:31 (NIV)

The word "Lent" comes from the Old English word "lencten," which means "springtime" or "lengthening of days."[2] Even better, the purpose of Lent is found in the person of Jesus. He is the point and must be our priority. Today, we're looking at a guy by the name of Levi, a tax collector who had a decision to make.

When Jesus approached Levi, the man could only see two options: stop and listen but change nothing, or ignore Jesus and continue moving about his community collecting taxes. But Levi was compelled by an invitation: "Follow me!" Lent season requires an intentional response to the invitation of Jesus to *follow*. Levi's reaction was swift and immediate.

"And Levi got up, left everything and followed him." — Luke 5:28 (NIV)

Levi left practices, vocation, and former ways of life to follow Jesus. His "followership" led to discipleship, and his discipleship led to service and evangelism. How do we know? Verse 29 says Levi held a banquet that gathered a large crowd of tax collectors who came to hear Jesus. You see, Levi said *yes* to the Lord and gave others the chance to do so as well. So, what will you do today? Maybe you're saying, How can I focus on Jesus when I'm at work? How can I do what I'm being asked to do while I'm busy with other things? I'm glad you asked.

First, accept the invitation daily to follow Jesus — not by accident but by intent. Start your day by following Jesus in silence and solitude; follow Him in a focused time of worship, prayer, and His Word. Next, follow Him out your door to the places where Jesus has directed your day. As you're in the marketplace, open your eyes to see where He's leading and to whom He's leading you.

Additional Reading

Isaiah 58:9b-14   Psalm 86:1-11

Lord, May I respond to Your invitation to follow You today. Open my eyes that I may not miss any opportunity to allow You to use me to draw others to Yourself.

In Jesus' Name, Amen.

Day 5

First Lenten Sunday

God is Ever Present

Minister Lisa Purville

Today's Reading
Mark 1:9-15

"And a voice came from heaven: 'You are my Son, whom I love; with you I am well pleased.'"
— Mark 1:11 (NIV)

In my walk with Christ, I've learned that my greatest accomplishments are often followed by the greatest challenges. Yet, the most outstanding prize is knowing I never have to walk through any troubles alone. This biblical passage tells of a similar experience.

Mark's first chapter details an incident before Jesus' ministry when He got baptized; the Son of God was immediately commended by His Father. Can you imagine the genuine sense of satisfaction and joy Jesus must have experienced knowing He had pleased His Father? Then, at once, He was led to the wilderness to be tempted by the devil. *Talk about coming down off an accomplishment high real fast.* Yet, God remained. We know this because God knew exactly when and where to comfort and restore Jesus after He survived His time of testing without falling to temptation. And in response, Jesus went on to proclaim the Good News!

When you are faced with a challenge after a great success, it can feel like a blow to your ego. You may wonder if you are truly capable of handling the pressure and maintaining the level of excellence that brought about the success in the first place. But like Jesus, you must remember that you are never alone. Your faith in God can sustain you through any trial, and you can emerge stronger and wiser on the other side.

Though it may seem daunting, remember that the pressure you feel is merely a testament to how God has brought you to victory in the past. Those successes have set the bar high because you have proven your faith and God's faithfulness to overcome any obstacle. This new challenge is an opportunity for you to further hone your skills, expand your knowledge, and redefine what it means to achieve greatness.

Additional Reading

Genesis 9:8-17   1 Peter 3:21   Psalms 25:3

Father, I pray to be constantly aware of your faithfulness. In trials, I ask that Your Spirit remind me of Your presence. I will look at my setbacks as opportunities to trust you more. Thank You, Father, for being sovereign over it all. Amen.

Day 6

First Lenten Week: Monday

Delight To Do Good

Minister Dario Lariosa

Today's Reading
Matthew 25:31-46

"'Truly I tell you, whatever you did for one of the least of these brothers and sisters of mine, you did for me.'"
— Matthew 25:40 (NIV)

One of the key messages of the *Parable of the Sheep and Goats* is for God's people to love others. The "good works" mentioned in this parable are not the cause of salvation but the effect of salvation. Good works in a believer's life are a direct overflow of our love for God and love for others. Believers will treat others with kindness and a sincere desire for the happiness of others. Sacrifice means giving something up for the sake of something of higher value. As believers, can we be willing to fast from the familiar and comfortable to be involved in random and intentional acts of kindness and service to others? Separating goats from sheep would have been a common practice for those listening to Jesus tell this story. Jesus used this familiar practice to make a point about humanity being goats or sheep. The hard truth is that sheep are those who have accepted alvation in Jesus, and the goats are those who have rejected Jesus as their Lord and Savior. Theologian Charles Spurgeon summarizes his parable:

"When they stand before the judgment-seat, the bare idea of there being any excellence in what they have done will be new to the saints, for they have formed a very lowly estimate of their own performances, and what they have done seems to them too faulty to be commended. The saints fed the hungry and clothed the naked because it gave them much pleasure to do so. They did it because they could not help doing it, their new nature impelled them to it. They did it because it was their delight to do good and was as much their element as water for a fish or the air for a bird. They did good for Christ's sake, because it was the sweetest thing in the world to do anything for Jesus."[3]

We must ask ourselves, are we living a life of service towards others? Are we showing love and compassion to those around us? The Parable of the Sheep and the Goats reminds us that these actions are not optional but essential to our faith. As Spurgeon eloquently stated, the saints fed the hungry and clothed the naked not because they wanted recognition or praise, but because it was their delight to do good and serve Jesus.

Additional Reading

Leviticus 19:1-2, 11-18   Psalm 19:7-14

Heavenly Father, Help me live a life of service towards others and show love and compassion to those around me. May I be like the sheep who hear Your voice and follow You, serving others with joy and gladness.
In Jesus' Name, Amen.

Day 7

First Lenten Week: Tuesday

Check Yourself

Minister Shauniqua Coty

Today's Reading
Matthew 6:7-15

"And when you pray, do not keep on babbling like pagans, for they think they will be heard because of their many words."
— Matthew 6:7 (NIV)

We all need check-ups! Regular examinations help us to keep track of how we are spiritually, physically, emotionally, and socially. Of course, doctors can help us with the physical, yet we need some check-ups for the sake of maturing. As believers, we have the Holy Spirit, who helps us peel away the layers of our sinful characteristics and replace them with Christ-like qualities. Unfortunately, too often, we recognize how much other people should change and ignore our need for transformation. The Holy Spirit seeks to produce characteristics representative of Jesus (e.g., the Fruits of the Spirit). Jesus made it clear in Matthew 6:7 that the Sadducees and Pharisees were guilty in two areas regarding their prayer lives: The spiritual leaders sought selfish glory and vain repetition. They wanted to impress people with their prayers. Have you ever done the right things for the wrong reasons? What is a multiplicity of words that don't reach our heavenly Father's heart? Haven't we all been guilty of having wrong motives?

The Holy Spirit has your best interest at heart, so if you suspect your prayers are sometimes self-seeking, *check yourself.* Whether in prayer or other areas of your daily walk, check and correct your motivation. Ask God to search you and see if there is any wicked way in you. Ask the Lord to lead you in the way everlasting. For a proper check-up, check in with the Lord daily; submit and sacrifice to the glory of God alone.

As you engage in this daily check-up with the Lord, remain vigilant against the subtle temptations that may lead you astray. Sacrifice your own agenda and preferences, setting aside personal gain for the sake of aligning your life with His divine plan. Let go of all selfish motives and allow the Holy Spirit to transform your heart so that it reflects the selflessness and love exemplified by Christ.

Additional Reading

Isaiah 55:6-11   Psalm 34:15-22

Father, Help me to take a look at who I am, and make me willing to check my moves and my motives so that Your glory can be revealed in me and through me.

In Jesus' Name, Amen.

Day 8

First Lenten Week: Wednesday

Remain in My Love

Minister Reggie Alvarez

Today's Reading
John 15:1, 6-16

"Live in me. Make your home in me just as I do in you. In the same way that a branch can't bear grapes by itself but only by being joined to the vine, you can't bear fruit unless you are joined with me."
— John 15:4 (MSV)

When you sit down to read and reach up to turn the switch on the lamp beside your chair, what do you do if the light does not come on? You probably let out a sharp sigh, raise yourself from your armchair, and trace the cord to the wall to check that it's plugged in. In John 1, Jesus tells us how important it is for believers to stay connected to the Father — our Source. When we do not remain attached to our Source and become separated from God, we are rendered useless and unproductive, just like an unplugged table lamp. However, when God and His words flow, we will be productive, receiving whatever we ask in His name. All we need to do is remain in His love.

John 15:5 shows us God's desire to have an intimate and organic relationship with us. To be intimate is to remain close, faithful, and devoted to God and the things of God. To be organic means that our relationship with God must be essential, natural, and harmonious. When we remain connected to God intimately and organically, His joy becomes our joy (John 15:11). We can ask for whatever we want because we will find our requests to be harmoniously aligned with His will. We will be in tune with God when we love, pray, and serve. Let's remain in God's love, so we can continue to be productive in Him.

But let us not forget the practical aspects of remaining connected to God. Just as a lamp requires a power source to illuminate the darkness, so too do we need to remain plugged into the source of all light and life. We must nurture our relationship through acts of love, prayer, and service. These are the conduits through which we receive the abundant grace and wisdom needed for fruitful living.

Additional Reading

Acts 1:15-26   Philippians 3:13-21   Psalm 15

Father God, Thank You for being the source of my life. Keep me intimately and organically at home in Your love so that Your joy becomes mine. My heart's desire is to remain in Your love and will. In Jesus' Name, Amen.

Day 9

First Lenten Week: Thursday

Relational Persistence

Dr. Onorio Chaparro

Today's Reading
Matthew 7:7-12

"For everyone who asks receives; the one who seeks finds; and to the one who knocks, the door will be opened."
— Matthew 7:8 (NIV)

How do you respond when someone greets your requests with silence, delay, or rejection? The response of silence can be tough to deal with. Silence can trigger our insecurity or be interpreted as contempt or indifference. But is that what we do to others? What if the quality of our relationships affects our ability to receive from God? Our attitude determines our approach, and our approach determines success or failure, correct? So, what does this have to do with prayer?

First, Jesus promises that if we ask, seek, and knock, we will receive a positive response. Prayer is the gift of access, but our persistence is rooted in our beliefs. Second, our earthly experiences do not define the benevolence of our Heavenly Father. Some families and communities hurt their children. But God is good all the time and has our best interests at heart. Do you lower your expectations in prayer? Knowing God wants the best for you, what would keep you from asking for the best?

Too often, we don't ask because we prefer to be self-sufficient or fear disappointment. Maybe we don't pray because we are distracted by social media, trials, or troubles. Knocking implies diligence and shows we are looking for God's response in the day-to-day. Asking, seeking, and knocking isn't just about receiving but also being a blessing to others. Are you a good gift to others? Jesus tells us to ask, seek, and knock; this isn't just about our private life with God. Instead, we are to be proactive agents of God to others. Whatever you want for yourself, find ways to give those things to others. As Minister Aaron Jenkins reminds us, "Got needs? Sow seeds." Is it time to knock on the door of an estranged family member or friend? Ask how you can bless your neighbor. Seek the good of others.

Additional Reading

Genesis 15:1-6, 12-18   Psalm 138

Heavenly Father, I come to You with humility, hope, and trust. I embrace Your call and seek Your face with all my heart. I knock with anticipation and faith, knowing that answers will come in Your time and wisdom. In Jesus' Name, Amen.

Day 10

First Lenten Week: Friday

Recognizing the Heart of Sacrifice

Pastor Jamaal Bernard

Today's Reading
Matthew 5:20:20-26

"For I tell you that unless your righteousness surpasses that of the Pharisees and the teachers of the law, you will certainly not enter the kingdom of heaven."
— Matthew 5:20 (NIV)

As our Lenten journey progresses, delving deeper into the notion of sacrifice for our faith, it becomes paramount to comprehend the essence of Jesus' teachings. In Matthew 5:20, He imparts upon us the imperative to transcend the mere adherence to rules akin to the Pharisees. Rather, our focus should lie within the recesses of our hearts.

To truly grasp the significance of this message, we must explore beyond the surface level of religious observance. It is not enough to perform rituals dutifully or recite prayers mechanically. Instead, we are called upon to cultivate a profound transformation within ourselves, in both thought and deed.

The Lenten season affords us a sacred opportunity for introspection and self-examination. As we engage in acts of sacrifice and penance, we are challenged to strip away the superficial layers that veil our true intentions. It is through this process that we begin to understand the concept of sacrifice on a much deeper level.

Sacrifice, in its purest form, emanates from a place of genuine love and devotion towards God and humanity. It requires us to relinquish our selfish desires and replace them with selflessness. When we approach sacrifice from this perspective, it becomes a conduit for spiritual growth and enlightenment.

During these forty days of Lent, we find solace in knowing that through sacrifice, we align ourselves more closely with Jesus' teachings. We embark on a sacred pilgrimage towards as our actions become an embodiment of our innermost faith.

In sacrificing material comforts, we awaken a heightened sense of gratitude for what truly matters in life – the bonds of love and compassion that connect us all.

Additional Reading
Ezekiel 18:21   Psalm 130

Dear God, Help me understand that true righteousness comes from the heart. Change me from the inside, make me more like Jesus. Help me seek reconciliation and live out my faith with love and sincerity.
In Jesus' Name, Amen.

Day 11

First Lenten Week: Saturday

All We Need is Love

Minister Mischa Field

Today's Reading
Matthew 5:43-48

*"But I tell you, love your enemies and pray for those who
persecute you..."*
— Matthew 5:44 (NIV)

Jesus tells us to love our enemies, and we spend a lifetime looking for loopholes. Maybe love is a far-off goal. Perhaps He only meant our enemies within our friend group. Maybe it's just on weekends and holidays. Part of the problem is that we don't understand clearly the definition of love. We think it's a feeling, and we're not feeling it. The word Jesus used, however, was "agape." It is God's transcendent love for humanity. And it extends all the way to those who persecute us. Jesus made these our prayer assignments. God's love is intentional and sacrificial. It's a choice to benefit someone else at our own expense. God's love is redemptive. It chooses to see the best in people and seek the best for them. God's love is patient, kind, selfless, and forgiving. It extends grace and pursues peace, even though it is not deserved. That is how God treats us. Jesus said,

"Love your enemies and pray for those who persecute you, that you may be children of your Father in heaven. He causes his sun to rise on the evil and the good and sends rain on the righteous and the unrighteous" (Matthew 5:44-45).

Every day of our lives, we receive love we do not deserve, love we have not earned and cannot earn. And that means that love may not look how we expect it to. Loving our enemies means praying for their good instead of rooting for their demise. It means seeing their humanity against every self-righteous impulse to villainize them. Now, seeking the best for someone may mean that love isn't always warm and fuzzy. It may require boundaries. It may require tough conversations. Love is not easy. But love never fails (1 Corinthians 13:8).

Additional Reading

Deuteronomy 26:16-19   Psalm 119:1-8

Father, help me to love my enemies today. Help me to see them as You do: broken and beautiful. Let me believe for their growth, and root for their victory. I pray in Jesus' Name. Amen.

Day 12

Second Lenten Sunday

Surrendering Self for Divine Promise

Minister Adam Durso

Today's Reading
Mark 8:31-38

"For whoever wants to save their life will lose it, but whoever loses their life for me and for the gospel will save it."
— Mark 8:35

On this faith journey, Jesus challenges us to take up our cross and follow Him. It's not easy - we have to make sacrifices that might seem overwhelming. But these sacrifices hold the key to true life and lasting fulfillment. So let's push aside the distractions that hinder our spiritual growth. In a world full of noise and chaos, we must find peace in solitude and seek solace in silence to allow God's word to speak to our hearts and minds. Dive into the living, breathing word of God. Let it be your guide, teacher, and companion n this surrender-filled pilgrimage toward divine promise. Within ts sacred pages lies the strength and wisdom we need to face any bstacles ahead. Open your heart and mind to its transformative ower. As you completely surrender yourself to God, you'll see the nbreakable connection between surrender and divine promise. In noments of doubt or confusion, turn to the scriptures for guidance nd find comfort in the stories of those who walked before us - David, Moses, and Abraham.

n Genesis 17 we witness the unfolding of a divine covenant between God and Abraham. Like Abraham, we too are called to surrender ourselves completely to God's plan. We may encounter mountains of uncertainty and valleys of despair along our faith journey. But it is hrough surrender that we find the strength to climb those mountains nd emerge triumphant from the darkest valleys. Remember that urrender is not a sign of weakness; it's an act of deep trust in a God vho always knows what we need.

Additional Reading

Genesis 17:1-7, 15-16   Romans 4:13-25   Psalm 22:22-30

Loving Father, As I embrace the challenges of self-surrender, strengthen my faith and help me trust in Your promises. May my willingness to lose my life for Your sake lead to the discovery of abundant life in Christ.
In the Name of Jesus, Amen.

Day 13

Second Lenten Week: Monday

A Leading with Love

Minister Malissa Redmond

Today's Reading
Luke 6:27-38

"But to you who are listening I say: Love your enemies, do good to those who hate you, bless those who curse you, pray for those who mistreat you."
— Luke 6:27-28 (NIV)

Have you ever wondered how people extend unconditional love and compassion to deliberate offenders? The complicated exchange of emotional and mental anguish can undoubtedly frustrate the process of following Christ. Above all, as believers, we are expected to demonstrate the love of God without exclusivity to those we consider the easiest to love. I've marveled at one of Jesus' greatest lessons in adversity: showing loving kindness to those who intentionally caused harm with false accusations, persecution, or maltreatment. As an example, we see the redeeming love of Jesus displayed on Calvary's cross despite the hostility towards him by relentless religious leaders who coerced crowds of people to justify their sinful practices. He taught in Luke 6:37-28, saying, "But to you who are listening I say: Love your enemies, do good to those who hate you, bless those who curse you, pray for those who mistreat you."

Reflecting on Jesus' instructions provokes deep thought concerning matters of the heart and repentance, whether you're offended or the offender. Dr. Martin Luther King and Mahatma Gandhi were known for their profoundly beautiful contributions to fighting hatred under great hostility; they chose the path of peace until the bitter end. Martin Luther King Jr. said, "Darkness cannot drive out darkness; only light can do that. Hate cannot drive out hate; only love can do that."[4] What an unfathomable statement!

May Psalm 79:8 - 9 be our heart's cry —

"Let Your compassion and mercy come quickly to meet us, For we have been brought very low. Help us, O God of our salvation, for the glory of Your name; Rescue us, forgive us our sins for Your name's sake" (AMP).

Additional Reading

Isaiah 58:1-9   Psalm 51:1-10

Heavenly Father, Help me to show Your love in dark places. Grant me wisdom and peace to walk in the light even when it's uncomfortable. Soften my heart so that I may honor You.
In Jesus' Name, Amen.

Day 14

Second Lenten Week: Tuesday

Sacrificial Service

Minister Paul H. Coty, III

Today's Reading
Matthew 23:1-12

"For those who exalt themselves will be humbled, and those who humble themselves will be exalted."
— Matthew 23:12 (NIV)

Have you ever experienced the embarrassment of sitting in a movie theater or at some event only to find out you were in the wrong seat? Being removed and redirected, especially to a less enviable area, makes the blunder even more uncomfortable. If something similar has happened to you, I'm sure it was just human error, but imagine assuming a position you know belongs to someone else and then being called out and removed. It would be humbling — humiliating.

In Matthew 12, Jesus begins a dialogue as He observes the Pharisees. He says, *Listen to them, but don't do what they do.* The Pharisees pridefully exalted themselves to seats they reserved for themselves while denying positions to those who may have needed them most. There is nothing like the sin of pride.

Pride promotes itself while denying others; humility denies self and promotes others. A manifestation of pride is putting the self on display. Jesus calls us to put ourselves on hold for the benefit of others. The root of humility is love. Love doesn't boast and is not prideful; it honors others and is not self-seeking (1 Corinthians 13:4-5).

Properly put, pride serves itself, and love serves others. How will you serve differently during this season? Is there a population that the Lord calls you to serve? Perhaps you need to put something aside to focus on others. Is the Lord asking you to back up so others can go before you? Could He be asking you to sacrifice buying your next gadget and instead sow into the Kingdom of God? In what ways can you deny your desire to serve those less fortunate? The call to serve is not a mere suggestion but a divine beckoning from the Lord Himself. What ways can you deny yourself so that you might serve others?

Additional Reading

Isaiah 1:2-4, 16-20   Psalm 50:7-15, 22-24

Lord, I repent for the ways I've preached more faith than I have lived. Help me to humble myself and honor You through sacrificial service to others.

In Jesus' Name, Amen.

Day 15

Second Lenten Week: Wednesday

God's Point of View

Minister Lisa Purville

Today's Reading
Matthew 20:17-28

*"...whoever wants to become great among you must be your servant,
and whoever wants to be first must be your slave..."*
— Matthew 20:26-27 (NIV)

My most important goal is to live by God's point of view daily, which means to speak and act in a way that pleases Him. In that pursuit, I'm often confronted with the truth that my way of doing and seeing things is not God's way. This passage reminds me of that, as the mom of James and John asks a question that she believes she is entitled to ask; Jesus quickly shows her she is wrong.

So often, we can mistake hard work and outstanding leadership with grand egos, pomp, and power, which is how James, John, and their mother believed. Yet, in God's kingdom, a great leader is one who is humble, overlooked, and, by outward appearances, seems owerless. If given a choice, I choose God's style of leadership, vhich may make me appear unassuming, and I am okay with that. believe so often in this world, people work hard for grand rewards .nd elevation to power. Yet, instead of serving the people they are 'esponsible for, they laud power over them.

esus is the most excellent example of how someone who had it all vas willing to give it up, serve, and die for us all. As I think about this eason of lent, I do so with a desire to be conscientious and serve hose around me with graciousness and humility. I seek to use the ime to search my heart to see what things I need to give up or let ;o of to become more like the ultimate servant leader, Jesus Christ.

ust as Jesus laid down His life for all humanity, Lent challenges us o reflect upon how willing we are to sacrifice for the greater good. iacrifice can manifest in many ways - giving up our time for someone n need, extending forgiveness to those who have wronged us, or olacing the needs of others above our own.

Additional Reading

Jeremiah 18:1-11, 18, 20   Psalm 31:9-16

Father, As I grow in knowledge and understanding, I pray that it will always be coupled with humility. Point out things I need to set aside so that I can hear from You. Help me be quick to serve those I am called to lead without ego.
In Jesus' Name, Amen.

Day 16

Second Lenten Week: Thursday

A Litmus Test

Minister Dario Lariosa

Today's Reading
Luke 16:19-31

"I the Lord search the heart and examine the mind, to reward each person according to their conduct, according to what their deeds deserve."
— Jeremiah 17:10 (NIV)

Jesus' story in Luke 16 has been used to teach about heaven and hell and to rebuke the wealthy; the lesson being *either you will own your money, or it will own you.* Where we spend our money shows what we value. Every receipt reveals what we really care about. Sacrifice is surrendering something without thinking of getting it back, detaching ourselves from self-centeredness. It brings us to a place of unselfish love. Sacrifice leads to service that fosters love, care, and concern for your neighbor.

This parable also reminds us that it's human nature to live as the wealthy man did, knowing who needs help but unwilling to do anything about it. The parable serves as a wake-up call to individual believers and the church corporately. We must act with compassion

Compassion recognizes the suffering of others and then takes action to relieve that suffering. Compassion embodies a tangible expression of love, especially for those who are struggling and hurting. Compassionate people sometimes make difficult choices, accepting risks many would never take and giving what most would hold on to. Compassionate people reach out and touch when most step back with arms folded. Compassion and celebrity don't mix.

Love isn't interested in receiving loud applause; instead, incredible acts of compassion might never be known by others.[5] Professor Peter Gurry, a renowned scholar and expert in biblical teachings, captures the essence of this parable: "A heart unwilling to help others—because it might be risky, or they might not deserve it, or it might cost us too much—is a heart unwilling to recognize the desperate help we ourselves need from God."

If you hesitate in reaching out to others because of fear of risk, doubts about deservingness, or concerns about personal cost, remember your own desperate need for God's help.

Additional Reading

Jeremiah 17:5-10   Psalm 1

Dear God, Please help me to test my motives and intentions and be honest with myself. Give me strength to act with compassion, kindness, and love towards others, even in difficult times.
In Jesus' Name, Amen.

Day 17

Second Lenten Week: Friday

Until the Time Comes

Minister Shauniqua Coty

Today's Reading
Matthew 21:33-43

*"The stone the builders rejected has become the cornerstone;
the Lord has done this, and it is marvelous in our eyes."*
— Matthew 21:42 (NIV)

For everything in life there is a time and a season. Some seasons we welcome, others we'd rather pass us by as quickly as possible. The phrase 'Time is of the essence', reminds us that timely performance is an essential obligation and failure to perform in a timely manner can result in disappointment, breach or loss.

Over time, we can be found awaiting our season to change, while the season was specifically and intentionally assigned for you for your learning, growth, maturity, perseverance and building of your faith. We want God's perfect timing, but when will we embrace it so that God can mold us and fashion us for our good and for His glory. It is clear in the *Parable of the Tenants* (Matthew 21:33-43), that the tenants whom the vineyard was rented to had a specific assignment. The tenants were to care for the vineyard until it was harvest time. Unfortunately, when harvest time came, the fruit was not made available as it should have been. When the landowner sent his servants to collect the fruit from the tenants, his tenants appeared to have a different agenda. The time had come, but the servants weren't found occupying as the landowner had instructed. Just like many of our assignments have been clearly given by God, and yet we get off task — possibly due to a change in season. Don't let your season cause you to be detoured by hurt, fear, greed, temptation, pride, for these obstacles sometimes come as a set up to keep us from finishing our assignment.

Until the time comes for your harvest, be a good steward of what is entrusted to you, know that God has equipped you for His work in each season, and trust that God's timing is perfect, until He comes.

Additional Reading

Genesis 37:3- 4, 12-28   Psalm 105:16-22

Father, Help me to stay focused on Your purposes and to push through when opposition rises against me. Keep me mindful of the times and seasons so I don't miss any opportunity to serve Your Kingdom. In Jesus' Name, Amen.

Day 18

Second Lenten Week: Saturday

Everything I Have is Yours

Minister Reggie Alvarez

Today's Reading
Luke 15:11-32

"as far as the east is from the west, so far has he removed our transgressions from us."
— Psalm 103:12 (NIV)

G*ive me my share now!* This is our introduction to the younger son we would come to know as "the prodigal" (Luke 15:12). Jesus tells the story of two sons, one demanding his portion of his father's estate. Then, in just a few short verses, we are given insight into how he squandered his inheritance. After being at his lowest, the young man comes to his senses and returns home, hoping to be accepted as a servant. Instead, he is met with open arms of a loving father and a celebration —with gifts! The older brother believed he deserved rejection, but received restoration. Can you relate to this story?

Many of us have, at one time, fallen away from Christ, living recklessly before coming to our senses, turning back to the Father, nd being forgiven. We know what it is to be welcomed into open rms of love. Now, let's look at the other son — the one who stayed.

Considering he was always faithful to his father, can you understand his anger? *The one who left with an entitled attitude gets the party? How is this fair?* Well, here is the plot twist: After the older son onfronts his father about all the attention his younger brother is getting, the father says, "You are always with me, and everything I have is yours." In other words, *Yes, your brother was enticed by the lust of the eyes, the flesh, and the pride of life. Your brother was lost, but now he is found. Now, he can finally feel the acceptance you have experienced every day.*

Although one brother felt entitled and the other felt overlooked, there was grace and love for both sons. Everything they ever needed was in their father's loving arms. The beautiful lesson for you is this: Another person's blessing will never rob you of your own. Our Father has all the love and forgiveness the world will ever need.

Additional Reading

Micah 7:14-15, 18-20   Psalm 103:1, 12

Father God, Thank You for Your unconditional love that meets me where I am. Never let me forget that everything I ever need — peace, love, joy, hope, happiness, fulfillment — all of it is found in You. In Jesus Name, Amen.

Day 19

Third Lenten Sunday

Protect Your Space

Minister Mischa Field

Today's Reading
John 2:13-22

"For the message of the cross is foolishness to those who are perishing, but to us who are being saved it is the power of God."
— 1 Corinthians 1:18 (NIV)

Lent invites us to consider our ways. Are our habits healthy? Are our mindsets right? How can we get closer to God? These are questions of boundaries. God demands priority in our lives. Some spaces belong to Him alone. We should worship the Lord and Him alone. We should pray to Him, and Him alone. In study, we must not allow other voices to compete with His authority. In church, we must gather as the body and not as a business network. There are times to read other books and places to do business; However, not on God's time or in God's space.

Jesus confronted a violation of boundaries when He went to the temple in Jerusalem before Passover. Because people came from great distances (Galilee was 90 miles away), they couldn't always bring their sacrifices with them. So, vendors were on-site selling animals for sacrifices. Because pilgrims from other countries needed currency exchanged for the transaction, they money-changers were also set up to do business within the temple gates. The vendors and the money changers were facilitating business, which would not be a problem, except they were doing it in the worship space. The one place designated for prayer had become the mall, so Jesus drove them out. Sometimes, He must do the same with us.

We lead hectic lives. We are constantly looking to streamline. Cutting corners with people brings immediate, tangible consequences, so we are more likely to cut corners with God. We give Him less time. We give Him divided attention. You may think, *I can do two things at once.* Perhaps you can multitask — but should you? Are you giving God your best or just giving Him what's left? It's not enough to do the right thing. We also need to do it in the right way. Some spaces are for God alone.

Additional Reading

Exodus 20:1-17　　　1 Corinthians 1:18-25
Psalm 19

Father, Help me honor You with my boundaries today. Remove every distraction that drowns out Your voice. Reveal to me the idols that divide my loyalty. Remind me to reserve Your space for You alone. I pray in Jesus' Name, Amen.

Day 20

Third Lenten Week: Monday

Challenging Prejudices

Minister Adam Durso

Today's Reading
Luke 4:23-30

"Truly I tell you," he continued, "no prophet is accepted in his hometown.
—Luke 4:24

Have you ever faced rejection in your life? It can leave you feeling alone, unsure of yourself, and defeated. Jesus understood this all too well. When visiting His hometown, Jesus faced rejection as He challenged their preconceptions. The rejection He faced was not a minor inconvenience, but a testament to the strong prejudices and doubts in His community. Picture the scene as Jesus stands in the synagogue to share His wisdom and grace. As He begins to speak, skepticism washes over the crowd. They struggled to reconcile who they thought He was with the profound words coming from Him. Doubts crept in, casting shadows on their hearts.

But despite this rejection, Jesus remained resolute in His mission to bring transformation and enlightenment to all who would listen. His power transcended human understanding and could conquer even the strongest prejudices. This power brings comfort and hope to us in our own experiences of rejection. Doubt, a common companion to rejection, often creeps its way into our hearts and minds, leaving us vulnerable and questioning our worth. Yet, Jesus' resolute spirit teaches us that doubt does not have the final say.

In moments when you find yourself grappling with doubt and questioning your worth, it is crucial to remember the unwavering resolve that Jesus exhibited in the face of rejection. In moments when doubt threatens to consume us, we can find strength in His example. We can reflect on His journey, from the moment He was rejected by society to the moment He transcended human understanding through His teachings and miracles. In His resilience lies the blueprint for conquering doubt.

So, when you find yourself at a crossroads, grappling with uncertainty and questioning your worth, take solace in Jesus' resolute spirit. Embrace that inherent power within you that knows that doubt does not have the final say.

Additional Reading
2 Kings 5:1-15b   Psalm 42:1-7

Compassionate God, Help me to recognize and confront my prejudices. May the spirit of Christ guide me to embrace those who are different from me, remembering that in diversity, Your beauty is revealed. Amen.

Day 21

Third Lenten Week: Tuesday

Grace to Forgive

Minister Malissa Redmond

Today's Reading
Matthew 18:21-35

"Then Peter came to Him and asked, 'Lord, how many times will my brother sin against me and I forgive him and let it go? Up to seven times?' Jesus answered him, 'I say to you, not up to seven times, but seventy times seven.'"
— Matthew 18:21-22 (NIV)

The beautiful exchange between God and humanity is graciously displayed through the precious gift of salvation. What a costly, loving sacrifice that continually reveals Jesus' commitment to the redeeming love of the Father. Many times in life, we encounter opportunities to share this same love with others. When we struggle to extend grace to others, we are reminded of our frailties and desperate need for wisdom, patience, and grace. The gospels show us that Peter needed reminding at times.

Peter's dominant personality was revealed during a heightened time of adversity involving a certain servant of the High Priest. Peter cut off the Roman soldier's ear when they came to arrest Jesus (Matthew 6:51-55). The Lord responded with healing and instruction, showing no animosity even to the one who betrayed Him (Matthew 26:50), as an example of His earlier teaching on forgiveness.

Consider a time when you were faced with an opportunity to extend forgiveness but wondered if your heart was in the right place. Did you overlook the offense or were you tempted to hold a grudge? Did you hear our loving Savior's words echo in your heart to respond according to the scriptures?

As you navigate this labyrinth of emotions, you must remember that forgiveness does not necessarily imply forgetting or condoning the actions that caused you pain. Instead, it is a conscious choice to release yourself from the shackles of resentment and open your hearts to healing. Psalm 25:3-10 says, "Show me your ways, Lord, teach me your paths. Guide me in your truth and teach me, for you are God my Savior, and my hope is in you all day long." May this word rejuvenate your mind and empower you with grace today.

Additional Reading

Daniel 3:1-30   Psalm 25:3-10

Lord, Help me to walk in the light of Your word and extend grace as You've shown me time and time again. Search my heart; You know my motives and lead me in the path of righteousness.
In Jesus' Name, Amen.

Day 22

Third Lenten Week: Wednesday

Believe Every Word

Minister Paul H. Coty, III

Today's Reading
Matthew 5:17-19

*"For truly I tell you, until heaven and earth disappear, not the
smallest letter, not the least stroke of a pen, will by any means
disappear from the Law until everything is accomplished."*
— Matthew 5:18 (NIV)

A contract is legally binding. In sports management, if a new
owner takes over a particular team; the contract of each player
must be honored. The agreement must be fulfilled even if that player is removed from the team. Whatever the contract states must be
kept regardless of leadership changes. The Pharisees believed that
Jesus had come to undo the law and dismantle the contract that
they had with God. In Matthew 5:17, Jesus cleared up that misun-
derstanding.

Jesus had not come to dismantle the contract but to honor it to the
full. Often, we misinterpret circumstances that appear to have come

to destroy us; instead, God's purpose through those times is to build us up. Jeremiah 29:11 says, "I know the plans I have for you says the Lord. Plans to prosper you and not to harm you. To give you a hope and a future."

The Lord watches over His Word to perform it during this and every season. He cannot act apart from His Word. He is not a man and cannot lie (Numbers 23:19). As the Father sensitizes your heart through the Lenten season, you'll recognize the many ways Jesus is honoring the contract, fulfilling His promises and purposes in your life.

Through prayer and reflection, you will come to see how God's promises are being fulfilled in your life. Perhaps it is through unexpected blessings that leave you in awe of His provision. Or maybe it is through challenging circumstances that ultimately lead you toward growth and transformation. Whatever the case may be, Jesus remains steadfast in His commitment to fulfill His promises and purposes.

Additional Reading

Deuteronomy 4:1-2, 5-9   Psalm 78:1-6

Lord, Please give me eyes to see, ears to hear, and a heart to receive Your truth. Thank You for Your faithfulness, that I can trust You to do what You say and be who You say You are.
In Jesus' Name, Amen.

Day 23

Third Lenten Week: Thursday

Walking the Talk

Minister Lisa Purville

Today's Reading
Luke 11:14-23

"Obey me, and I will be your God and you will be my people. Walk in obedience to all I command you, that it may go well with you."
— Jeremiah 7:23 (NIV)

A s a Christian, I have a desire to see my friends saved and in a growing relationship with Jesus Christ. It is important to me that my profession about the Good News lines up with my actions on a daily basis. It's also important that when I fall short, and my actions and words are inconsistent with the Gospel, I acknowledge that, take responsibility, humbly repent, and ask for forgiveness. In other words, I don't want to be double-minded or like a house that is divided. I want to make sure that my actions are in line with what I know to be true by way of the presence of the Holy spirit inside of me. In this passage, Jesus said that if one goes against oneself, they undermine and weaken their position — a house divided against itself can't stand (Mark 3:25).

I must not say I believe one thing and do another. I can't say I'm a follower of Christ and do something in complete opposition to that declaration. My mind, will, emotions, and actions have to be on one accord and constant with God's right way of doing things. One of the things about Jesus is that He was consistent. He obeyed the Father and was about His Father's business in everything that He said and did. Our walk must be the same.

Jesus tells us that we are with Him or against Him. There is no in-between. Do you choose to be with Him? Decide that your words and actions will be aligned with God's way, even if that means you need to let go and give up your current pattern of thinking and behavior. And when you fall short, choose repentance and forgiveness.

Additional Reading
Jeremiah 7:23-28   Psalm 95:6-11

Father search my heart and see if there is any thought, emotion, or habit that is not in line with your way of doing things. Help me in my desire to not be double minded, so that I can live a life that is consistent with your Word, your Truth, and your Life. Amen.

Day 24

Third Lenten Week: Friday

Vertical and Horizontal

Minister Dario Lariosa

Today's Reading
Mark 12:28-34

"'Love the Lord your God with all your heart and with all your soul and with all your mind and with all your strength.' The second is this: 'Love your neighbor as yourself.'"
— Mark 12:30-31 (NIV)

When a teacher of the law heard the Sadducees debating with Jesus and the wise responses they were given, he wanted to know the most important commandment. Jesus answered by quoting Deuteronomy and Leviticus, which tell us to love God and love others.

The word *love* is greatly misunderstood and often abused. Many believe it is nothing but an emotion. However, *love* is the ability to give at the expense of self; it is sacrificial. Theologian CS Lewis said, "Love is never wasted, for its value does not rest upon reciprocity." More than affection, love is an unwavering commitment centered in our will— a commitment to the vertical (love of God) and the orizontal (love for others). To love God is to passionately pursue Him with our total being (heart, soul, mind, and strength). I humbly submit to you that to love God with your entirety is to begin to see God as Savior, where your life is lived in obedience and gratitude. To love God with your total being is to start to see God as your sustainer, where you begin to curb your enthusiasm to curse, you begin to respond and not react to the body blows that life hits you with, and you start submitting your gifts, talents, and abilities for Him to use.

The vertical fills us with what we need for the horizontal. To love your neighbor is to compassionately seek their well-being, imitating God by taking their needs seriously. Your neighbor is everyone in need. Love thinks in terms of responding abundantly. Love refrains from exploitation. To claim to love God while not loving people (or vice versa) is a contradiction. Theologian Paul Tripp says, "You can't look horizontally for what you will get only vertically, and you can't wait vertically for what you have been called to do horizontally."

Additional Reading
Hosea 14:1-9   Psalm 81:8-14

Father, Thank You for the love and grace You have bestowed upon me. Help me to love others as You have loved me. Fill me with Your love so that I can love others without hesitation and without boundaries.

In Jesus' Name, Amen.

Day 25

Third Lenten Week: Saturday

Humility All Day, Everyday

Minister Shauniqua Coty

Today's Reading
Luke 18:9-14

*"For all those who exalt themselves will be humbled, and those who
humble themselves will be exalted."*
— Luke 18:14 (NIV)

Living in a time when people are quick to judge based on limited
information has often led to presumptions and inaccurate judgments. The time needed to find the truth about a person or situation
requires unbiased discernment; sadly, many of us are quick to slap
on labels without a moment's thought that we may have misinterpreted the signs. Author Bonnie Lyn Smith advises, "Ask if you need
to, but don't assume. Sometimes our bad feelings are only assumptions and speculations doing dark dances in our heads." If you were
to see a church member in the company of the town drunk, where
would your mind go? Jesus was faced with that type of judgment
from the Pharisees.

In Matthew 9:10-17, we have a glimpse of Jesus being about the Father's business in the company of well-known exploiters and iniquitous individuals. Religious leaders poorly assessed the reason for the gathering, assuming He couldn't have a good motive for being with those types of people. The Lord responded to their questions with laser-focused clarity, confidence, and correction, saying, "Those who are healthy have no need for a physician, but [only] those who are sick. Go and learn what this [Scripture] means: 'I desire compassion [for those in distress], and not [animal] sacrifice,' for I did not come to call [to repentance] the [self-proclaimed] righteous [who see no need to change], but sinners [those who recognize their sin and actively seek forgiveness]" (Matthew 9:12-13, AMP).

Jesus sacrificed His reputation to offer forgiveness to those in need regardless of the backlash. He refused to conform to the pressure within the culture to avoid certain people because people were His purpose. Do you recognize the same to be true for you? Stay focused on your assignment. You will certainly face significant challenges; however, stay the course, finish well, and never hesitate to offer grace to those in need.

Additional Reading
Hosea 6:1-6   Psalm 51:15-20

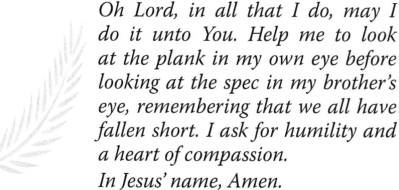

Oh Lord, in all that I do, may I do it unto You. Help me to look at the plank in my own eye before looking at the spec in my brother's eye, remembering that we all have fallen short. I ask for humility and a heart of compassion.
In Jesus' name, Amen.

Day 26

Fourth Lenten Sunday

Shine Your Light On 'Em

Minister Reggie Alvarez

Today's Reading
John 3:14-21

"But the one who practices the truth comes to the Light, so that his deeds will be revealed as having been performed in God."
— John 3:21 (NASB)

Many years ago, I worked for a textile business in the garment district of New York. One of my roles was to examine fabrics on the fabric inspection machine. This machine is used to check fabrics for any defects such as stains, rips, holes, and spots. Attached to the machine is a backlight that highlights the flaws. My employer told us not to use the light. He intended to hide the flaws, deceive the customers, and sell at top dollar. However, when I ran the fabric for customers, I would turn the backlight on because I did not want to operate in deceit. You could say I would *shine the light on 'em*. As you can imagine, my employment there did not last long.

Do you remember the day you said *yes* to Jesus? Do you recall when the scales fell from your eyes, and you became cognizant of your sins, flaws, and defects?

In John 3:19 Jesus speaks of light and darkness as opposing forces in the world. He explains that His purpose is not to judge us, but rather to guide us towards salvation. However, He acknowledges that some individuals may be drawn towards darkness due to their immoral actions. Despite this, Jesus offers an open invitation for anyone seeking to leave behind darkness and embrace the light of God's love.

When we choose to live in the light, we are surrendering ourselves to God's plan. Truly, it takes courage to stand up for righteousness in a world filled with moral ambiguity. But as followers of Christ, it is our duty to bravely exemplify what it means to live in the light so others can see Christ in us. Be bold and courageous and shine your light on 'em.

Additional Reading
Numbers 21:4-9   Ephesians 2:1-10
Psalm 107:1-3, 17-22

Father God, Thank You so much for being my Way, my Truth, and my Life. You are the light of men. I commit to continually practicing truth by walking in that light, giving You all the Glory.
In Jesus' Name, Amen.

Day 27

Fourth Lenten Week: Monday

Believing is Seeing

Minister Mischa Field

Today's Reading
John 4:43-54

"It will also come to pass that before they call, I will answer; while they are still speaking, I will listen."
— Isaiah 65:24 (NASB)

Faith stretches us. It is, in the words of Hebrews 11:1, the substance of things hoped for, the evidence of things not seen. We believe for unseen things which will materialize in unknown ways. Sometimes, God shows up immediately. Sometimes, we wait. By faith, though, we believe the promise of Romans 8:28, that all things are working together for our good. As we grow in faith, we must sacrifice our demand for proof. In John 4:43-54, Jesus came to the region of His birth, Galilee, observing that a prophet gets no honor in His hometown. However, the people welcomed Him, as they had seen Him perform miracles.

urthermore, Jesus went to Cana, where He turned water into wine
t a wedding. That's where He met an official with a sick son, who
begged Jesus to come to heal him. Jesus said, "Unless you people
see signs and wonders, you will never believe" (John 4:48). The
official, however, had already exercised a fair amount of faith. He
had enough faith to travel sixty-four miles to find Him, and he had
enough faith to beg the Healer to do it. With Jesus' assurance that
his son would live, the man headed home. That's faith in action. Still,
like most of us, he wants to verify the miracle.

When his servants told him his son was alive, he asked when it
happened. When the timing lined up with his interaction with Jesus,
he believed — he and his entire household. Walking by faith bears
fruit. Still, it's a process. The journey to healing may combine faith
that takes action with a need to question until the proof arrives. By
faith, however, we believe that it will.

Additional Reading

Isaiah 65:17-25   Psalm 30:1-6, 11-13

*Father, Help me to trust You today,
even when I cannot see You working.
Before any miracle, or spectacle, or
manifest provision, let me receive
Your Word. And let it be enough.
I pray in Jesus' Name. Amen.*

Day 28

Fourth Lenten Week: Tuesday

Healing Waters of Grace

Minister Adam Durso

Today's Reading
John 5:1-18

"When Jesus saw him lying there and learned that he had been in this condition for a long time, he asked him, 'Do you want to get well?'"
—John 5:6 (NIV)

Have you ever needed healing? In the Bible, we learn about a man who suffered for many years. He felt hopeless and didn't know if he would ever get the help he needed. Everything was about to change for this man — on that day, Jesus came by the pool and asked one direct question with a profound purpose — "Do you want to get well?"

The question was not simply to ascertain the man's desire for healing; indeed, Jesus knew everything. Instead, His question served as an invitation, a call to action requiring the man to confront his willingness to embrace the transformative power of divine grace.

In our lives, we often find ourselves in similar predicaments - trapped by circumstances, burdened by ailments of body or spirit. We must ask ourselves if we are truly ready to surrender to the healing power that awaits us. Just as the man at Bethesda had suffered for 38 long years, you may have endured your own struggles for what feels like an eternity. Yet, precisely within these trials, your faith is being tested and refined.

Jesus' miracle in Bethesda was not merely a physical cure but a representation of His limitless compassion and unwavering love. In that moment, the man's faith aligned with the divine will, allowing for the miraculous restoration of his body and spirit.

Let this story serve as a reminder that when you stand at the precipice of healing, you must be a willing participant in your own redemption. Respond today to Jesus' call with unwavering faith and humility, placing your trust in His infinite wisdom.

Additional Reading

Ezekiel 47:1-9, 12   Psalm 46:1-8

Gracious Healer, Pour out Your healing grace upon me. Like the man at Bethesda, I desire to experience the transformative power of Your love, bringing wholeness to my brokenness. Amen.

Day 29

Fourth Lenten Week: Wednesday

Living by Example

Minister Malissa Redmond

Today's Reading
John 5:19-29

"Sing for joy, O heavens, and exult, O earth; break forth, O mountains, into singing!"
— Isaiah 49:13 (ESV)

As a parent for thirty-two years, I often give thought to my journey, which was filled with unforgettable moments that inspired lifelong change in many ways. One of my greatest joys is watching my children develop their personal relationships with God because of the foundation laid from childhood. I'm also grateful to witness my eldest daughter's parenting skills. She blessed us with three incredibly beautiful girls who benefit significantly from her personal devotion to the Lord. They, too, are learning about Jesus and serving in their church because of her example. John 5:19-20 says, "Jesus gave them this answer: 'Very truly I tell you, the Son can do nothing by himself; he can do only what he sees his Father doing, because whatever the Father does the Son also does. For the Father loves the Son and shows him all he does. Yes, and he will show him even greater works than these, so that you will be amazed."' What an extraordinary moment where Jesus communicates His faithfulness to the Father.

The blueprint for modeling life in Christ, especially in front of your children, includes praise, bible study, prayer, worship, thanksgiving, and serving others.

"All Your works shall give thanks to You and praise You, O Lord, And Your godly ones will bless You. They shall speak of the glory of Your kingdom And talk of Your power, To make known to the sons of men Your mighty acts And the glorious majesty of Your kingdom. Your kingdom is an everlasting kingdom, And Your dominion endures throughout all generations." — Psalm 145:10-13 (ESV)

Who wouldn't serve a God like this?

Additional Reading

Isaiah 49:8-15   Psalm 145:8-19

My Father and God, I give You thanks and praise for Your faithfulness throughout generations. Help me to exemplify character and shine Your light at home and to the world. In Jesus' Name, Amen.

Day 30

Fourth Lenten Week: Thursday

All Roads Lead to Jesus

Minister Paul H. Coty, III

Today's Reading
John 5:30-47

"You search the Scriptures because you think they give you eternal life. But the Scriptures point to me!"
— John 5:39 (NKJV)

I do a lot of traveling with my work. My travels take me to different places across the United States, some places I have been before, others new to me. As I drive, I pay attention to the signs from each point of the journey to my ultimate destination. Life gives us signals, as well. We can miss them if we're not paying attention. Jesus pointed the way, but the Pharisees missed the point.

The Pharisees were highly respected scholars, well-versed in their ancestors' laws and customs. Despite their knowledge, they failed to truly understand the profound message hidden within their sacred texts.

ust as we pay attention to road signs while driving, we must also
sten to the signs that guide us toward a deeper relationship with
esus. These signs are not just abstract ideas; they are present in
very aspect of our lives, from studying scripture to praying. Every
assage in the Bible reveals something about Jesus, showing us His
ivine nature and eternal purpose. And each prayer is a direct line
f communication with Him, bringing us closer to His endless grace
nd love. But faith without action is like a sign on the road — it may
oint us in the right direction. Still, unless we follow it, we will never
each our destination.

Vatch for evidence of God's hand on your life in ordinary
ircumstances as you make your way through your day. But don't
mit yourself to the big once-in-a-lifetime moments. Keep your eyes
pen and appreciate the little miracles woven into everyday life.

Additional Reading

Exodus 32:7-14   Psalm 106:6-7, 19-23

Dear God, Guide and direct me in Your ways. Help me make wise choices that honor You. Fill me with Your Holy Spirit, and be with me every step of the way. In Jesus' Name, Amen.

Day 31

Fourth Lenten Week: Friday

Growing Far

Minister Lisa Purville

Today's Reading
Luke 2:41-52

"Who am I, Sovereign Lord, and what is my family, that you have brought me this far?"
— 2 Samuel 7:18 (NIV)

In my walk with God, I've learned that growth is not an overnight process. This totally makes sense since even Jesus took time to grow. I've also learned that sometimes you must move in the opposite direction of those closest to you to follow Christ. This was evident in this passage in Luke as Jesus left His family so that He could go to His Father's house.

What I love most about this story is that Jesus didn't allow His family or age to get in the way. In this season in my walk with Christ, I am determined to pursue Him even if it means I must lose relationships or let go of things that are near and dear to me. Growth in my connection with Christ is my top priority. I am determined to not let anything, or anyone get in the way of me serving and growing with the Lord. I also understand that as I walk with Christ, I will eventually advance in knowledge and understanding. I must be mindful that I don't become arrogant. I want to grow like Jesus did.

The Lord's journey was not without its challenges, but His determination to listen, ask questions, and remain obedient to His parents paved the way for His growth and wisdom. His vast knowledge did not make Him arrogant or closed off to the teachings of others; instead, it fueled His hunger for learning and understanding.

I believe a person who stops listening and asking questions is determined to stay stuck where they are. This season let's press on with an open heart, mind, and willingness to learn from others.

Additional Reading

2 Samuel 7:4, 8-16   Romans 4:13-18
Psalm 89:1-29

Father, Help me to walk humbly with You. As I grow in knowledge and understanding, I will remain obedient to Your will and way. I pray I will not allow pride to creep up as I get wiser.
In Jesus's Name. Amen

Day 32

Fourth Lenten Week: Saturday

Drink If You Dare

Minister Dario Lariosa

Today's Reading
John 7:37-52

"Whoever believes in me, as Scripture has said, rivers of living water will flow from within them."
— John 7:38 (NIV)

The *Feast of Tabernacles*, was a celebration of how God provided water to Israel in the wilderness while on their way to the promised land of Canaan. On the last day of the commemoration, Jesus proclaimed to be the one who could satisfy their deepest thirst. Thirst indicates a lack of something, an emptiness that speaks to a need yet to be satisfied. Christ calls all of us to acknowledge this thirst and to quench and relieve it by drawing from a living well that will never run dry.

All our attempts to satisfy this thirst by some other means will meet dissatisfaction. To be satisfied means we are not yearning for something else. Satisfaction is gained by believing in the Lord and experiencing the indwelling of the Holy Spirit.

The Holy Spirit convicts nonbelievers of their sins. He also helps believers stay holy when they are tempted to sin. Conviction is vital for change. The Holy Spirit brings comfort to followers of Jesus. Still, the goal of the Holy Spirit is not to make us comfortably complacent.

Satisfaction in Christ will make us distinct from others. Has your dedication to the Lord required you to separate yourself from others in your life (John 7:40-44)? Satisfaction in Christ alone is a call to sacrificial living. Ask yourself, Am I willing to die to myself and live for Christ serving others? Let this be your clarion call: "All of me to all of you, O God, because of Jesus."

Additional Reading

Jeremiah 11:18-20   Psalm 7:6-11

Dear Lord, Thank You for all You have blessed me with. Guide me in serving others with compassion, and patience. I pray that my service brings joy and comfort to those in need, and that it may inspire others to do the same.
In Jesus' Name, Amen.

Day 33

Fifth Lenten Sunday

Losing to Win

Minister Shauniqua Coty

Today's Reading
John 12:20-33

"Anyone who wants to serve me must follow me, because my servants must be where I am. And the Father will honor anyone who serves me."
— John 12:26 (NLT)

No one wants to lose. We set out to win and consider losing to be a bad thing. When we fall short, we feel bad or think something's wrong with us when we lose that job, relationship, or friendship. However, successful men and women realize that with the correct response, loss can be a direct route to learning, maturing, and ultimately taking home the prize. We must be willing to lose what isn't working to make room for what will. Remember what Jesus told Philip and Andrew?

"Those who love their life in this world will lose it. Those who care nothing for their life in this world will keep it for eternity."
— John 12:25 (NLT)

o love our lives and all in it more than Jesus is to love amiss. Jesus isn't telling us to hate our existence; He is saying we must make our election sure and make a choice. It is impossible to fully embrace the Lord if things of the world are of higher priority.

Matthew 6:24 says, "No man can serve two masters: for either he will hate the one, and love the other; or else he will hold to the one, and despise the other. Ye cannot serve God and mammon" (KJV). Earlier in the passage of John 12, Jesus used an analogy of a seed that must "die" for its purpose to be fulfilled. As followers of Christ, we must be willing to lose everything to have everything; we ought to put 100% of our attention, urgency, and value into the will of God. It's our reasonable service and willing sacrifice.

Additional Reading

Jeremiah 31:31-34   Hebrews 5:5-10
                        Psalm 51:1-13

Heavenly Father, Help me give up whatever keeps me from You; there's truly no loss when I'm gaining more of You. Thank You that there is only freedom for those in Christ Jesus, and may I make room for that which You have prepared for me, in Jesus' Name, Amen.

Day 34

Fifth Lenten Week: Monday

The Verdict

Minister Reggie Alvarez

Today's Reading
John 8:1-11

"Neither do I condemn you; go and sin no more."
— John 8:11 (NKJV)

The *Bureau of Labor Statistics* reports that "Judges typically do the following: research legal issues; read and evaluate motions, claim applications, and legal briefs; listen to arguments by opposing parties; determine whether information presented supports a charge, claim, or dispute and decide whether procedures are being conducted according to the law. It is the responsibility of a Judge when presiding over a trial, to ensure fairness and that the jury arrives at a decision in correct fashion."[7]

Our society tends to move quickly and publically to judge someone accused of immoral behavior. Our ruling is delivered through mean posts and cruel memes on social media to late-night jokes until — yep — *canceled*. Our *Cancel Culture* criticizes and casts stones like we have each forgotten our faults and failures. In John 8, we read the account of religious leaders and Pharisees bringing before Jesus a woman caught in adultery. They wanted to hold court in front of a crowd and challenged Jesus to cast judgment on her. But here is the truth: they cared nothing for the woman; they were only using her to trap Jesus into saying something incriminating so they could cancel Him. But Jesus flips the table on the accusers.

"...let the one who has never sinned throw the first stone!" — John 8:7 (NLT)

One by one, they left. Where they wanted a guilty verdict, Jesus instead showed compassion and gave the woman new life, saying, "Go and sin no more." As believers, it is crucial to consider the wisdom and care that Christ shows to sinners. When others bring people to the courtroom of public criticism, let us ensure that our verdict reflects His wisdom and compassion.

Additional Reading

Genesis 38:1-30   Psalm 23

Father God, Your Word reminds me in Titus 3:5 that You saved me, not because of my works in righteousness, but according to the mercy, love, and compassion You showed me. Thank You for reminding me to show others the same. In Jesus' Name, Amen.

Day 35

Fifth Lenten Week: Tuesday

Believe

Dr. Onorio Chaparro

Today's Reading
John 8:21-30

"'Who are you?' they asked. 'Just what I have been telling you from the beginning,' Jesus replied."
— John 8:25 (NIV)

When we are sick or heartbroken, where do we turn? We turn to who or what we trust. After God freed Israel from slavery, they wandered in the wild. Why? God wanted to build their trust. On one occasion, the people got impatient and railed against God and Moses. The result? God judged their unbelief by sending serpents. What was the solution? Moses hung a bronze serpent on a pole, allowing anyone bitten to look up in faith for healing. The remedy was trust in God.

In John 8:21-30, the unbelieving people confronted Jesus because they didn't believe that He was of divine origin. Lent reminds us of the more profound mysteries of our faith. First, the Scriptures and Christian doctrine require lifelong study in a posture of humility and worship. Second, Jesus claimed an intimacy with the Father that superseded anyone else. Jesus' authority flowed from His intimate knowledge of the Father. You can read an author's words, but you will not know the writer like his child knows him. Finally, in today's passage, Jesus stressed the importance of trusting Him. The consequence of rejecting Jesus' divine nature and unique relationship with the Father is eternal separation from God. Jesus reminds us that, just as Israel needed to look up, we must look to Him, hung on a cross for the world's sins, to escape judgment and find healing.

Lent is a season to remember the great lengths the Lord went to for our salvation. There is only one way to receive this gift — Jesus is the one way. To reject Jesus is to be in danger of judgment. Lent helps us to live intentionally, renouncing presumption, and affirm our belief that Jesus is the source of our salvation. Will You turn and trust in Jesus?

Additional Reading

Numbers 21:4-9   Psalm 102:15-22

Dear God, Help me to see You for who You truly are. You are the source of all goodness, merciful, compassionate, and just. Help me to trust in Your promises, to follow Your commands, and to seek Your will in all things. In Jesus' Name, Amen.

Day 36

Fifth Lenten Week: Wednesday

True Freedom

Pastor Jamaal Bernard

Today's Reading
John 8:31-42 (NIV)

"Jesus replied, 'Very truly I tell you, everyone who sins is a slave to sin. Now a slave has no permanent place in the family, but a son belongs to it forever. So if the Son sets you free, you will be free indeed.'"
— John 8:34-345 (NIV)

Today, in the heart of Lent, I challenge you to think about "true freedom" as described by Jesus in John 8:31-42. He emphasized that true discipleship involves adhering to His teachings, which leads to the ultimate freedom—liberation from the bondage of sin. This freedom is not about physical liberation but the profound spiritual freedom that comes from knowing and living in the truth of Christ.

In Daniel 3, we see a vivid demonstration of faith and freedom in God. Shadrach, Meshach, and Abednego face a life-threatening trial for their unwavering dedication. They are freed from the physical flames and the bondage of fear and earthly powers. Their story is powerful testament to God's deliverance for those who remain steadfast in their faith.

love what Psalm 150 teaches us. It calls us to praise God in all circumstances. This Psalm, full of joy and adoration, reminds us that our ultimate freedom lies not in evading hardship or escaping adversity, but in recognizing the sovereignty and grace of God in every circumstance. It is in steadfastly praising Him, without reservation or condition, that we unlock the chains that bind us to the world.

As we continue through Lent, let's meditate on the freedom Christ offers. It is a freedom from sin, urging us to relinquish our transgressions and seek His forgiveness. It is a freedom from fear, empowering us to cast aside the anxieties that weigh upon our hearts and trust in His providence. And it is a freedom from worldly constraints, calling us to shed the shackles of materialism and embrace a life marked by faith, worship, and adherence to His eternal truth.

Additional Reading

Daniel 3:14-20, 24-28   Psalm 150

Heavenly Father, This Lenten season reminds us of the true freedom that comes through Your Son, Jesus Christ. Help us to grasp the depth of this freedom, which liberates us from sin and empowers us to live in Your truth. In Jesus' Name, Amen

Day 37

Fifth Lenten Week: Thursday

The Great I Am

Dr. Onorio Chaparro

Today's Reading
John 8:51–59

"'Very truly I tell you,'" Jesus answered, "'before Abraham was born, I am!'"
— John 8:58 (NIV)

What if God was one of us? Joan Osbourne's 1995 song, *One of Us*, is a very cynical tune; some might say anti-Christian (or at least anti-Roman Catholic). "What if God was one of us; Just a slob like one of us; Just a stranger on the bus Tryna make his way home?"[8] It is unflattering to describe humans as slobs; however, the lyrics identify our great common denominator — we are all just trying to make it to where we belong. Sin caused us to be alienated from God and hostile toward others. Our greatest need is to be home with God. Abraham was looking for a home and an eternal heritage.

When Jesus claimed to fulfill what Abraham longed for and then promised that same gift to all who would keep His word, His opponents couldn't believe their ears! Then Jesus laid it out for them.

When Moses asked God's name, God responded, "I am who I am." God told Moses to tell Israel, "I am has sent me to you" (Exodus 3:13-15). Jesus was saying that the same Lord of Israel's exodus from Egypt was standing right in front of them. Jesus answered Osbourne's question. God became one of us in Christ Jesus. Jesus is the way to know God, to be at home with God, but also what it means to be truly human. Osbourne's song said humans were slobs and strangers, but in Christ, we are salt and light, royal priests, a holy nation. Jesus is the *I Am* for every human. In Christ, we discover the source of meaning, identity, fulfillment, purpose, etc. Jesus became one of us to save and restore us, and God would make His home with

Additional Reading

Genesis 17:1–8   Psalm 105:4–11

Heavenly Father, I am grateful that I am now Your child through the life, death, and resurrection of Christ Jesus. Help me to ground my identity, purposes, and destiny in Your grace and truth by the power of Your Holy Spirit.
In Jesus Name, Amen.

Day 38

Fifth Lenten Week: Friday

Follow the Map!

Minister Mischa Field

Today's Reading
John 10:31-42

"And in that place many believed in Jesus."
— John 10:42 (NIV)

Sometimes, we get mad at God for being exactly who He said He is. He is a healer. He is a provider. He is a redeemer. And because He is all that, some think He should be more — do more. We blame our choices on God. We think He should protect us from the consequences of our actions. We wonder why He allows certain things that are entirely of our making.

The exciting thing is that as God's son, Jesus did the works of His father. And we are sons and daughters of God. That means we should resemble Him and be recognizable as His. It means the works we do should be His work, even if it makes our critics uncomfortable. It also means He has given us power and authority to fix some messes ourselves, and we can walk in the power of the Spirit and the authority of our calling. When we talk about sacrifice, we acknowledge that there are things we need to surrender. God has put things in our hands that we haven't necessarily handled well. Lent gives us the opportunity to put them in the right place. We reorder, rearrange, recycle, repurpose, reposition, and retire. We may need to let God repossess some stuff that doesn't belong to us, like the keys to the car that He is to drive.

When we say, "Jesus, take the wheel," we must be prepared to go where He is going. But let us not forget that this act of surrender is not passive; it demands action on our part. If we desire to arrive at the destination God intends for us, we must follow Him faithfully. His footsteps become our guide and His teachings become our compass. We must set aside our own desires and comfort zones and courageously step into uncharted territory. But if we follow Him, we will also lead others to Him. And that will make the whole trip worthwhile.

Additional Reading

Jeremiah 20:7-13   Psalm 18:1-7

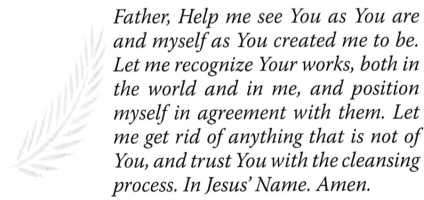

Father, Help me see You as You are and myself as You created me to be. Let me recognize Your works, both in the world and in me, and position myself in agreement with them. Let me get rid of anything that is not of You, and trust You with the cleansing process. In Jesus' Name. Amen.

Day 39

Fifth Lenten Week: Saturday

Broken Chains

Pastor Jamaal Bernard

Today's Reading
John 11:45-53

*"The stone the builders rejected has become the cornerstone; the
Lord has done this, and it is marvelous in our eyes."*
— Psalm 118:22-23 (NIV)

I'll forever cherish the moment I surrendered to Jesus. In an instant, fear, every chain holding me back, every binding force, was broken. The journey of surrendering to Jesus is a transformative experience that resonates deeply within the depths of our souls. As we let go of our fears and relinquish control, we find ourselves enveloped in the Father's loving embrace. It is through obedience that we begin to taste true freedom.

Jesus Himself exemplifies the power of surrender. In His willingness to lay down His life for us, He breaks the chains that bind us and offers us a pathway to salvation. His sacrifice is a beacon of hope, guiding us towards a life filled with purpose and meaning.

he Word of God echoes this call for obedient surrender throughout 's pages. It encourages us to yield ourselves to the loving authority f the Father, trusting in His wisdom and guidance. Through our rokenness, He forges breakthroughs - moments where we witness he miraculous transformation that can only occur when we urrender our lives completely to Him.

hrough the journey of brokenness, a path paved with hardships nd trials, the Father molds us into vessels of His grace and mercy. It ; in these moments of vulnerability that He forges breakthroughs, hattering the shackles that bind us and illuminating the path to niraculous transformation. As we surrender our lives fully to Him, Ie breathes life into our shattered pieces, molding them into a eautiful mosaic of redemption and restoration.

n our surrender, we discover that true strength lies not in control or elf-reliance but in vulnerability and dependency upon our Creator. Through submission, we become vessels for His love and grace to low through us, impacting our lives and those around us.

Additional Reading

Ezekiel 37:21-28   Psalm 118:1-2, 19-29

Lord, Help me understand my purpose and to share Your message with everyone You called me to reach. Help me communicate truth in love without judgment or compromise.
In Jesus' Name, Amen.

Day 40

Palm Sunday of the Passion

Your King is Coming to You

Pastor Jamaal Bernard

Today's Reading
Mark 11:1-11

"Hosanna! Blessed is he who comes in the name of the Lord! Blessed is the coming kingdom of our father David! Hosanna in the highest heaven!"
— Mark 11:9-10 (NIV)

As the citizens of Jerusalem eagerly awaited a political leader to overthrow the oppressive Roman Empire, their hopes were fulfilled in an unexpected way. Mounted on a humble colt, Jesus fulfilled the prophecy spoken by Zechariah centuries before. The words of Zechariah 9:9 resonated deeply with the people witnessing this extraordinary event.

"Rejoice greatly, O daughter of Zion! Shout aloud, O daughter of Jerusalem! Behold, your king is coming to you; righteous and having salvation is he, humble and mounted on a donkey, on a colt, the foal of a donkey..."

It was a profound moment, one that transcended the boundaries of earthly power and revealed a truth far more significant than any political revolution could offer.

The Triumphal Entry was not just a display of authority but an embodiment of divine purpose. Jesus' choice to enter as a humble servant on a simple colt highlighted His righteousness and the salvation He offered to all who believed in Him. In this unexpected manner, God's plan unfolded before their eyes, revealing that His answers often come in ways we least anticipate. As we commemorate Palm Sunday, let us remember that Jesus is our true King and we are citizens of His kingdom. Let us also never forget that Jesus came not to be served but to serve and give His life for ours. As citizens of His kingdom, it is our duty to embody His teachings and live lives characterized by love, compassion, and selflessness.

Additional Reading

Isaiah 50:4-9a   Philippians 2:5-11
Psalm 118:1-2, 19-29

Lord God, On this Palm Sunday, we reflect on the path Jesus willingly took, which led to His death on the cross for our salvation. Help me to grow and learn from Christ's example of humility and obedience. In Jesus Name, Amen.

Day 41

Holy Week: Monday

You Don't Know Like I Know

Minister Mischa Field

Today's Reading
John 12:1-11

*"For this reason Christ is the mediator of a new covenant, that those
who are called may receive the promised
eternal inheritance..."*
—Hebrews 9:15 (NIV)

People may not understand the things we do for love. They will not understand our joy in liberty if they have not known our bondage. If they have not owed our debts, they will not comprehend our gratitude toward the One who paid them. If they haven't experienced our pain, they will not grasp our resolve to avoid its source. And while our critics may be well-meaning, they may also have ulterior motives. Perhaps they feel convicted by our passion. They may be jealous of our devotion. If you're the smartest person in your group, you may need a new group, not just to keep growing but because your old group may reject you for doing too much. But Jesus affirms that our devotion is never too much.

In saying, "You will always have the poor among You, but You will not always have me" (John 12:8, NIV), Jesus does not minimize the importance of giving to people in need. Instead, He asserts the importance of worship. Faith without works is dead. Works without faith, however, is just us doing stuff without God. And we will soon run out of gas. Every trial in our lives has led us to this point. God allowed us to overcome hardship for a reason. He allowed us to experience bondage so we might know liberty. He allowed us to experience lack so we might appreciate abundance. He allowed us to be grounded with limitations so we could fly when He takes the limits off. *No limits*, however, does not mean *no critics*. When a crowd gathered to see Jesus and the resurrected Lazarus, the chief priests decided to kill Lazarus because he was drawing people to Jesus. Some people will want to kill us just for living. We might as well live.

Additional Reading

Isaiah 42:1-9   Hebrews 9:11-15
Psalm 36:5-11

Father, I will serve You with joy. May I never be so worried about people's opinions that I fail to heed Your voice. May I never give others the power to define, judge, or influence my faith. Today, help me to rest in You. Amen.

Day 42

Holy Week: Tuesday

Seeds of Sacrifice

Dr. Onorio Chaparro

Today's Reading
John 12:20-36

"Very truly I tell you, unless a kernel of wheat falls to the ground and dies, it remains only a single seed. But if it dies, it produces many seeds."
— John 12:24 (NIV)

Do you know your purpose? Lent reminds us that walking in our purpose means sacrificing to live in alignment with God. Jesus' mission had once focused on saving God's chosen people, Israel; at the point of today's text, God will glorify Himself through the Son by reclaiming all people into His family. Jesus sowed His life through death, like a seed, to reconcile all people back to God. Living in your purpose brings God glory.

We define purpose as the reason for which something exists or is done. Jesus fulfilling His purpose would bring forth God's glory. Glory is the intrinsic worth of something, but the process would not look glorious. We tend to attach glory to our achievements or omething sensational. In God's eyes, much of what we consider lorious is vanity. It would be on the cross, a tool of idolatry and ontrol, where Jesus would reveal the glory of God. The seed of His acrifice would reap a harvest we benefit from and will enjoy forever.

iving our purpose can be painful, and the process of glory requires acrifice. Jesus expressed His vulnerability and His victory to His isciples. You see, Jesus came to destroy the power and works of he devil. What power and works? The devil and his kin exploited uman sin, deceived nations, and assaulted God's image in people. esus' purpose was to judge the evil forces, strip them of their ower, and reclaim the nations. Jesus focused on His purpose, our beration, and the devil's damnation, and in doing so, manifested he glory of the Father. If we walk in God's light, we are dying to urselves so Christ can live through us. Your purpose is to answer he call to follow Jesus and see others freed from bondage to sin and ear of death. Until Christ returns, this is our purpose and how we ring God glory.

Additional Reading

Isaiah 49:1-71   Corinthians 1:18-31
Psalm 71:1-14

Lord of Glory, You designed me to love, enjoy, and glorify You. Forgive me for being easily distracted. By Your Spirit, help me to seek to bring You all the glory You deserve. In Jesus' Name, Amen.

Day 43

Holy Week: Wednesday

In God We Trust

Minister Mischa Field

Today's Reading
John 13:21-32

"Jesus said, 'Now the Son of Man is glorified and God is glorified in him.'"
— John 13:31 (NIV)

Relationships are spatial. The people closest to us have tremen dous power to bless us. They also have the greatest ability to hurt us. As He predicts His betrayal, Jesus is "troubled in spirit (John 13:21). Acknowledging or even realizing that we cannot trus a friend can be devastating. It hurts when we discover someone we have held close is unfaithful. If it's happening, however, God ha allowed it.

Sometimes, God will permit someone to disappoint us because we've placed them on a pedestal. As much as we expect family and friends to support us, no one is infallible. No person is our source No person is our rock. No person can "do anything but fail." No one but God, and He alone. God may allow a betrayal to occur and be revealed because we need to know those we labor amongst. Although it is painful, often it is the best thing a person can do for us — reveal themselves quickly. If a business partner has a gambling addiction, I'd rather know now than after ten years of building a business with them. Suppose your sweetheart has an anger management issue. In that case, you are better off learning it at the beginning of the relationship than after you are married with two kids.

Our theme this year is *sacrifice.* Have you ever had to sacrifice a dream when it revealed itself to be a fantasy — or a nightmare in the making? We may have to sacrifice opportunity when we learn it comes at a cost we were never designed to pay. God blesses and protects us both by giving to and taking things from us. Lent is a spiritual check-up, an annual doctor's visit that reveals the state of our health. And sometimes, a check-up identifies something that just needs to go.

Additional Reading

Isaiah 50:4-9a   Hebrews 12:1-3
                  Psalm 70

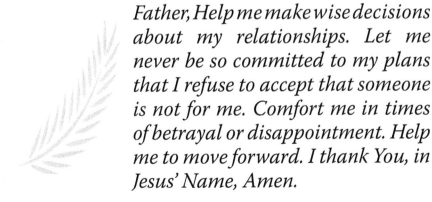

Father, Help me make wise decisions about my relationships. Let me never be so committed to my plans that I refuse to accept that someone is not for me. Comfort me in times of betrayal or disappointment. Help me to move forward. I thank You, in Jesus' Name, Amen.

Day 44

Maundy Thursday

Love Like Jesus

Dr. Onorio Chaparro

Today's Reading
John 13:1-17, 31b-35

"Now that I, your Lord and Teacher, have washed your feet, you also should wash one another's feet. I have set you an example that you should do as I have done for you."
— John 13:14-15 (NIV)

When was the last time you washed someone's dirty feet? When was the last time you had dinner with someone who was going to abandon you? Church hurt is real. Jesus experienced it after eating and washing the feet of His disciples. Today, a lot of people use their church hurt as a reason to abandon the church as an institution. But to be with Jesus means you and I are proactively and creatively loving our brothers and sisters in Christ. In Lent, today is Maundy Thursday.

The word "Maundy" comes from the Latin for *command (mandate)*. On this night, our Lord commanded His disciples to love one another as He loves. We also remember the last Passover meal our Lord shared with His disciples, where He instituted Holy Communion (the Eucharist or the Lord's supper). The communion table is a holy mystery that some Christians debate: *is it symbolic or spiritual?*

It is most important to come to the communion table, remembering His body and blood was a love sacrifice for His church. The mark of discipleship isn't how much we know but how much we love. The measure of Christian maturity is the degree to which we love the way Christ loved: redemptively, sacrificially, and faithfully.

Fortunately, our ability to love is in Christ and grows in us as we commune with Him. Christ shed His blood to forgive us, and we can find in Him the resources to forgive, serve, and love our brothers and sisters in Christ.

Additional Reading

Exodus 12:1-10, 11-15   1 Corinthians 11:23-26
Psalm 116:1, 10-17

Lord Jesus, Forgive me for using emotional wounds like disappointment and betrayal as excuses not to love the way You commanded. Help me to know that the fullness of my healing is in the faith to love others. In the Name of Jesus I pray, Amen.

Day 45

Good Friday

For Once and For All

Pastor Jamaal Bernard

Today's Reading
John 18:1 - John19:42

"When he had received the drink, Jesus said, 'It is finished.' With that, he bowed his head and gave up his spirit."
— John 19:30 (NIV)

Good Friday is a pivotal day in Christian faith, marking the crucifixion of Jesus Christ and His sacrifice for the sins of humanity. As we delve deeper into the narrative of John 18 and 19, we are confronted with the profound paradox of Good Friday. It is a day steeped in anguish and grief, where the weight of Jesus' suffering hangs heavy upon our hearts.

We witness the betrayal of Jesus by one of His closest disciples, Judas Iscariot. A kiss, once a symbol of affection and camaraderie, is now tainted by deceit and treachery. In those moments, the full weight of humanity's sin and brokenness pressed upon Jesus' houlders. He endured mock trials and false accusations with nwavering grace. The religious leaders jeered and spat at Him, heir hearts hardened with envy and fear of His teachings.

appeared that Jesus was at the mercy of His accusers, but we know he truth. Christ is not a victim in this narrative; He is in the hands f the same Father who holds our lives in His loving embrace. The uthority with which Christ submits Himself to this imminent uffering is not born out of weakness or defeat but rather an nwavering trust in God's plan for salvation. This sacrifice on the ross is a testament to His boundless love for humanity, offering us safe haven in the midst of life's storms.

emember that no matter what challenges or adversaries we may ace, there is one who holds ultimate authority over all things.

Additional Reading

Isaiah 52:13 - 53:12   Hebrews 10:16-25
Psalm 22

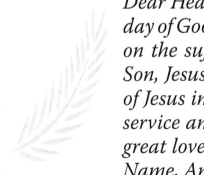

Dear Heavenly Father, On this holy day of Good Friday, I pause to reflect on the suffering and death of Your Son, Jesus Christ. May the sacrifice of Jesus inspire me to live my life in service and gratitude, honoring the great love You have shown. In Jesus Name, Amen.

Day 46

Holy Saturday

Practice Silence

Dr. Onorio Chaparro

Today's Reading
Matthew 27:57-66

*"In you, Lord, I have taken refuge; let me never be put to shame;
deliver me in your righteousness."*
— Psalm 31:1 (NIV)

Two thousand years ago, the day after Christ's crucifixion and burial was a Saturday — the Sabbath —and the enemies of Jesu were rejoicing over the illusion of their victory. The disciples were scattered, fearing for their lives and struggling with guilt and shame Other disciples waited for the first day of the week to visit the tomb and provide Jesus with the proper burial rites. What is this day supposed to mean for us? Holy Saturday is also known as the Grea Sabbath, Easter Eve, or Saturday of Light. Holy Saturday remember the burial of Christ's body in the tomb. Christians remember tha Jesus declared, "It is finished."

The grave was where the seed of His body was sown to rise in glory for our salvation. Christians wait together to celebrate Resurrection Sunday, the day of new creation and fresh beginnings. As God declared in Genesis on the first day of the week, "Let there be light," so too, Jesus, the light of the world, was brought from the dead. God raised His Son and started a brand new order that will culminate in His second coming. We await the ultimate new day when Christ returns.

Do you interpret God's silence as an opportunity to trust and rest, or do you get anxious? Do you know how to be still and know that God is in control when things don't go your way? In dark times, when we can't trace God's hand, you and I can trust God's heart. We can be free from our addictions and distractions in silence, knowing He is working everything out for our good.

Additional Reading

Job 14:1-14   1 Peter 4:1-8
Psalm 31:1-4, 15-15

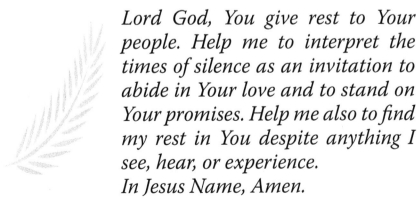

Lord God, You give rest to Your people. Help me to interpret the times of silence as an invitation to abide in Your love and to stand on Your promises. Help me also to find my rest in You despite anything I see, hear, or experience.
In Jesus Name, Amen.

Day 47

Resurrection Sunday

Celebrate!

Pastor Jamaal Bernard

Today's Reading
Matthew 28:1-10

"The angel said to the women, 'Do not be afraid, for I know that you are looking for Jesus, who was crucified. He is not here; he has risen, just as he said. Come and see the place where he lay. Then go quickly and tell his disciples: "He has risen from the dead and is going ahead of you into Galilee. There you will see him." Now I have told you."'
— Matthew 28:5-7 (NIV)

Resurrection Sunday, or Easter, celebrates the most momentous event in human history—the resurrection of Jesus Christ from the dead. Matthew 28:1-10 vividly describes the discovery of the empty tomb by Mary Magdalene and the other Mary, the angelic announcement of Jesus' resurrection, and the astonishing encounter with the risen Christ. What an experience and a joy it must have been to hear the good news that their Master — their friend — had risen from the dead.

In Romans, Paul describes how, through baptism, we are united with Christ in His death and, consequently, in His resurrection. This union with Christ signifies a transition from death to life, symbolizing our rebirth as Christians into a new life of righteousness.

Today, celebrate your deliverance from slavery to freedom. As you read Psalm 114, recognize yourself as a type of Israel being delivered from *Egypt* — the bondage of sin and hopelessness.

You have the promise of eternal life and earthly existence liberated from your sinful nature. This Easter Sunday, I challenge you to pause and thank God for all He has and is doing for you and your family.

Additional Reading

Romans 6:3-11   Psalm 114

Heavenly Father,

Today, I rejoice in the resurrection of Your Son, Jesus Christ. I am eternally grateful for the hope and life that His resurrection brings to our world.

Help me to truly grasp the magnitude of this miracle—the defeat of death and the promise of eternal life. May this understanding transform my life and inspire me to live with renewed faith, hope, and love.

As I celebrate this day, fill my heart with joy and my life with the light of Your presence. Guide me to share the good news of the resurrection with all I encounter. Thank you, Lord, for the gift of Your Son and the new life I find in Him.

In Jesus' Name, I pray. Amen!

Endnotes

1   "Bonnie Lyn Smith Quotes (Author of the Hills of Vincere Ridge)." *Goodreads, Goodreads, www.goodreads.com/author/quotes/9788043.Bonnie_Lyn_ Smith. Accessed 6 Dec. 2023.*

2   What is Lent? Lenten Meaning and Purpose Explained - Christianity. https://www.christianity.com/wiki/holidays/what-is-the-purpose-of-lent.html.

3   Spurgeon, Charles H. " Metropolitan Tabernacle Pulpit Volume 21 *The Final Separation." The Spurgeon Center, www.spurgeon.org/resource-library/sermons/ the-final-separation/#flipbook/. Accessed 6 Dec. 2023.*

4   King Jr., Martin Luther. *Strength to Love.* Harper & Row, 1963

5   Gurry, Peter. "Is the Rich Man and Lazarus a Parable?" *The Gospel Coalition, 28 Mar. 2019, www.thegospelcoalition.org/article/is-rich-man-and-lazarus- a-parable/.*

6   Lewis, C.S. "Love is never wasted, for its value does not rest upon reciprocity." *The Four Loves - Wikipedia*, Wikimedia Foundation, Inc., 9 Dec. 2023, en.wikipedia.org/wiki/The_Four_Loves.

7   Bureau of Labor Statistics, U.S. Department of Labor, Occupational Outlook Handbook, Judges and Hearing Officers, at https://www.bls.gov/ooh/legal/judges-and-hearing-officers.htm (visited *November 13, 2023*).

8   Osborne, Joan. "One of Us." *Relish*, Mercury Records, 1995, track 1.

Pastor Jamaal Bernard
Christian Cultural Center

Pastor Jamaal Bernard, a cultural strategist and innovative leader, is the Chief Operating Officer of Christian Cultural Center, embodying a vision of strong leadership intertwined with unwavering compassion. Simultaneously holding the position of Senior Pastor at CCC's Long Island Campus, he carries forward the legacy of his father, Reverend A.R. Bernard, who transformed a storefront ministry into New York City's largest church. Leading the movement of Unapologetic Ambassadors for Christ (UAFC), exemplifying a resolute stand for faith, Jamaal is also the author of "Unapologetic Christianity" and "Battle Rhythm," a vital resource empowering readers with practical insights. Passionate about sharing the love of Jesus, Jamaal and his wife Rita, married for over two decades, joyfully collaborate in ministry, raising five children: Kamryn, Stephanie, Jamall Jr., Liam, and Maali.

Christian Cultural Center
Christian Cultural Center, founded in 1978 by Rev. A. R. Bernard, began as a small parish in Brooklyn's Williamsburg neighborhood. With his wife Karen by his side, they spread the gospel of Jesus Christ and reached out to their local community. Today, CCC serves as a premier spiritual institution with campuses in Brooklyn, Long Island, and Orlando, Florida. CCC's mission is to spread the gospel of Jesus Christ, help spiritual seekers become transformed believers, and demonstrate the love and compassion of Christ to the world, through humanitarian works and social engagement.

About the Authors

Minister Mischa Field
Minister Mischa Field is an author and teacher who has served in ministry in Brooklyn for twenty-two years. He is the Director of Spiritual Life at *Christian Cultural Center*. A graduate of Amherst College and Alliance Theological Seminary, he finds consistent joy in uncovering the mysteries of faith and constant humility in attempting to practice them. His writing explores the intersections of divinity and humanity: faith, politics, identity, culture, and the soul. His book, "Soul of the Citizen: Prayers for a Divided Nation" was published in 2021. Born in Brattleboro, VT, Field lives in New York City with Lori, his wife of sixteen years and partner in ministry.

Minister Adam Durso
Expanding his ministry, Adam developed the Faith Breathes sermon series, reaching over 10,000 individuals globally each week with the transformative message of Jesus Christ. Rooted in his early walk with Christ, youth ministry remains a core passion. the Founder & CEO of Catalytic Consulting NYC, Minister Durso facilitates collaboration between seasoned and emerging leaders, offering leadership development training and consulting. Witnessing current and next generations thrive in life and leadership is a cornerstone of his ministry. Blessed with versatility, he's served in various capacities, including as a member of the New York Mayor's Clergy Advisory Council in the government space, on the ministerial team at Christian Cultural Center, and as President of LEAD.NYC for seven years, nurturing community leaders for the spiritual and social flourishing of greater NYC.

Minister Malissa Redmond

Malissa Redmond is a bestselling author, Brooklyn native, wife of three decades to her high school sweetheart, Derrick, and a mother and grandmother with an impassioned love for serving humanity. She serves on the ministerial staff of *Christian Cultural Center* through music, preaching, and teaching. In addition, she serves as an interfaith New York State Certified Chaplain providing pastoral care. Malissa is the president and CEO of *ForSmiles Inc.* a multifaceted consulting company, curating events, production and hospitality management. For the past three years, she's enjoyed supporting middle schoolers as the director of arts at a charter school in Brooklyn. She's an award winning artist who traveled the world ministering the gospel, appeared on many stages across the United States and touched many lives through venues like *Trinity Broadcast Network, The Today Show, Bobby Jones Gospel, Carnegie Hall,* and *Gospel Super Fest.*

Minister Paul H. Coty, III

Paul H. Coty III is the Vice-President of the Northeast Division of *Young Life.* This global para-church outreach introduces adolescents to Jesus Christ and helps them grow in their faith. Paul has 20 years of experience in the multi-ethnic ministry landscape. Paul exemplifies modern transformational leadership and innovation in urban ministry. Coty also has the privilege of serving as a minister at the *Christian Cultural Center* under the leadership of Pastors A.R. and Jamaal Bernard. Minister Coty is married to the gifted and anointed Shauniqua Coty and has the gift of 3 wonderful children: Paul IV, Jeremiah, and Savannah. Paul has spent the last 30 years in the service of Christ displayed through his work with men, young people, and the church.

Minister Lisa Purville

Lisa Purville has worked in finance for the last 20 years, helping clients achieve their financial goals. She graduated from the University of Maryland, College Park, majoring in Finance and minoring in African American Studies. She also holds her Master's in Christian Studies from Dallas Theological Seminary. Purville serves as a minister at *Christian Cultural Center*, where she re-enforces the values of faith, family, education, and community, as she provides spiritual guidance to people within the church community.

Minister Dario Lariosa

Born in Hawaii and raised in New York, Minister Dario spent many formative years in The Salvation Army. As a youth, he learned how to serve others discovered his passion for youth ministry and mission. In 1995, Minister Dario graduated from Nyack College with a degree in Communications. that same year, he became a member of *Christian Cultural Center.* While continuing his work with the Salvation Army, he served as a youth minister and youth camp program director before transitioning to Young Life, working as a youth center director in Jamaica, Queens. He is now the C3 University Youth and College Pastor and CCC Mission Director. Minister Dario has been blessed with 28 years of marriage to Lavern. Together, they are the proud parents of four children: Imani (27), Nia (21), Isaiah (19), and Joshua (15).

Minister Shauniqua Coty

Shauniqua Coty has served as a minister at *Christian Cultural Center* for over two decades. She is passionate about connecting people with God and encouraging believers to live out their faith. Shauniqua has worked in various ministerial roles within the CCC Ministry, including the C3 Youth Ministry, Missions Ministry, Remnant Step Ministry, and the Singles/Marriage Ministry. Serving and training young girls and women is her passion, ministering to them in creative, inspired, and life-changing ways. Shauniqua Coty has been a Speech Therapist for the New York City Department of Education for more than 25 years. Nothing compares to the joy and passion of her heart in sharing the Gospel of Jesus Christ, locally and abroad, so that the lost can be found and God glorified. She and Paul, her loving husband of 20 years, have three incredible, God-fearing children.

I wait for the LORD, my whole being waits, and in his word I put my hope.
— Psalm 130:5

Minister Reggie Alvarez

Reggie Alvarez is an ordained minister and youth leader at *Christian Cultural Center*. He is also a step dance director, choreographer, and missionary. Through his missionary travels from 1998 to 2003, Reggie helped establish over 8 multi-cultural step-ministries in over five countries: Holland, London, South Africa, Germany, and the Czech Republic. Reggie ministered with his Boots Step Ministry in Singapore, Guatemala, Jamaica, Puerto Rico, Mexico, and Uganda between 2004 and 2023. He has appeared locally on TBN, Gospel Superfest, the Universoul Circus, Carnegie Hall, and the Apollo Theatre. Boots has become known as a 'theatrical' and 'interactive' step-ministry. Today, under the leadership of Pastor A.R. Bernard and Pastor Jamaal Bernard, Reggie continues to conduct local outreach events and global mission opportunities, as well as minister the Word of God at CCC and C3 Youth Ministry.

Dr. Onorio Chaparro

Dr. Onorio Chaparro has been a son of the CCC ministry since 1996 and began full-time ordained ministry in 2005 after completing his Master's in Divinity from Princeton Theological Seminary. Through the years, Dr. Chaparro has served as director of the ICB Men's Ministry, the Spiritual Life Institute, and Connect Groups. He completed his Doctorate in Ministry in 2016 from Alliance Theological Seminary and is now part of the CCC Orlando church planting team. Dr. Chaparro is also the Associate Dean/ Director of Admissions at the New School of Biblical Theology, founded by Dr. A.R. Bernard. The best part of his life is being married to Adrienne A. Chaparro for over 23 years and raising their four dynamic children.

*I want to know Christ —
yes, to know the power of his
resurrection and participation
in his sufferings, becoming like
him in death, and so, somehow,
attaining to the
resurrection from the dead.*

— Philippians 3:10 -11

Printed in the USA
CPSIA information can be obtained
at www.ICGtesting.com
LVHW011640240224
772712LV00064B/1619